Walter Parke, Jospeph B. Williams

Gypsy Gabriel

A Romantic Comic Opera in Three Acts

Walter Parke, Jospeph B. Williams

Gypsy Gabriel
A Romantic Comic Opera in Three Acts

ISBN/EAN: 9783337103927

Printed in Europe, USA, Canada, Australia, Japan

Cover: Foto ©Thomas Meinert / pixelio.de

More available books at **www.hansebooks.com**

GYPSY GABRIEL.

A Romantic Comic Opera,

IN THREE ACTS.

WRITTEN BY

WALTER PARKE & WILLIAM HOGARTH.

COMPOSED BY

FLORIAN PASCAL,

London:

JOSEPH WILLIAMS, 24, BERNERS STREET, W.

CHARACTERS.

COLONEL TREMAINE, *Of Tremaine Hall* ....

HAROLD PENRAVEN, *Known as Captain Temple. The Lost Heir*...

DR. QUONDAM, *Tutor to Laura*

RICHIE ROLLESTON, *Farm-bailiff to the Colonel* ....

GABRIEL, *The Gypsy Chief* ....

SIMON GRIMSTONE, *Occupant of Penraven Castle*..................

BLACK RALPH, *A Smuggler* ....

LAURA TREMAINE, *Daughter of the Colonel* ....

DOLLY, *Her Attendant*...............

MRS. POLSWORTHY, *Widow Innkeeper*

SCENE.—*The Village of Tremaine, near Penraven Castle, Cornwall.*

PERIOD.—*End of 17th Century.*

SYNOPSIS.

ACT I.

THE village of Penraven. The rustic revels. The fierce COLONEL and the timid Tutor. GIPSY GABRIEL mobbed by the villagers and protected by RICHIE ROLLESTON. LAURA TREMAINE'S secret attachment. The loves of RICHIE and DOLLY. The legend of Penraven. The lost heir in disguise. SIMON GRIMSTONE'S evil schemes. GABRIEL and HAROLD in trouble. The attempted arrest. A rescue, and a bold escape.

ACT II.

VILLAGERS returning home. RICHIE befriends HAROLD. GABRIEL'S mysterious hints. He promises to tell HAROLD the secret of his birth. Tremaine Hall. The servants exposed to midnight terrors. HAROLD and RICHIE'S unexpected visit. Two serenaders, and four perplexed lovers. Dr. QUONDAM very much in the way. HAROLD and LAURA meet at last. GABRIEL reveals GRIMSTONE'S treachery. The COLONEL'S anger and astonishment. The intruders expelled from the Hall.

ACT III.

THE gypsy encampment in the ruined castle. BLACK
RALPH the Smuggler's secret interview with GRIMSTONE.
Plot to carry off HAROLD a second time. Dr. QUONDAM
protects the ladies. The COLONEL in ambush. GYPSY
GABRIEL throws off the mask at last, and denounces his
enemy GRIMSTONE. A desperate struggle. Retribution
overtakes the evil-doers. HAROLD's claim is proved, and
his wrongs righted. Conclusion.

GYPSY GABRIEL.

ACT I.

No. 1.—OPENING CHORUS OF VILLAGERS.

At evening, ere the set of sun,
  We take our turn of rest and pleasure,
For only those whose work is done
  Deserve or know the sweets of leisure ;
With sports upon the village green,
  With cheering songs and friendly glasses,
With whispered words of love between
  The blithe and comely lads and lasses ;—
    Dancing, flirting,
    So diverting
To the careless, gay, and young,
Fleet of foot and glib of tongue ;
For their elders pipes and ale,
Pleasant chat and mirthful tale ;
  Merrily each moment passes.
    When night grows dark,
      'Tis time to sleep,
    Till wakes the lark
      And sparrows cheep.
    When morning ray
      Gilds hill and plain
    Our working day
      Begins again.
And thus our humble lives are spent,
  Our duty well fulfilling ;
And those who talk of discontent
  Will preach to ears unwilling.

No. 1a.—CONCERTED PIECE AND SONG.

See, from the Hall comes Mistress Dolly!
  What is her errand? Where's she going?
She looks so sad, so melancholy
  She may have reason, there's no knowing.
Good morning, Dolly, what's the matter?

Dol.. I'll tell you, neighbours, if you stop your
    chatter.

SONG—"ACHES AND PAINS.

DOLLY.

I.

I'm going to see Dame Durden,
  And call on Gaffer Gray,
Who suffers from the rheumatic
  And cramp, by night and day.
I'll sit with Mother Mumble,
  Whose ague is so bad;
And Farmer Flip who used to drink
  Till now he's nearly mad.
Invalids complaining
  Of pain, and damp, and cold;
But some, I fear, are feigning,
  Such dreadful tales they told.
But small relief obtaining
  Because so poor and old.
Aches and pains, aches and pains,
  We are subject one and all,
  They may come to great and small,
  Who can tell what maladies may befall?

II.

I'm going to Willie Wilson,
  Who has a dreadful cough;
His baby brother is no more,
  The measles took him off.

While Gammer Gosling's lame,
    And cannot get about !
Her daughter has a quinsy,
    And her father's got the gout.
Patients loudly groaning,
    They make my blood run cold,
Such murmuring and moaning,
    And sorrows manifold.
Such maundering and droning,
    Then tales too often told.
Aches and pains, &c.

No. 2.—SONG.

RICHIE *and* CHORUS.

I.

RICH. I sing a song of Britons brave,
    And where's the nation braver ?
May Britain's flag for ever wave,
    But Britons never waver.
No flower can match the English rose,
    The rest are but pretenders ;
Confusion on our country's foes,
    And cheers for her defenders !

REFRAIN.

For ever may old England stand,
    As Freedom's staunchest friend ;
And may the glories of our land
    Increase and never end !

II.

I sing a song of sweethearts true,
    And wives the best and fairest,
If here or there's a scold or shrew,
    Such cases are the rarest.

May no one fear the truth to speak,
  Alike to friend and stranger ;
And may the strong protect the weak,
  Whenever they're in danger.

[Refrain as before.

No. 3.—BUFFO SONG.

Dr. Quondam.

I.

The heroes of the ancient time,
  The poets of the classic age ;
Their deathless deeds, their works sublime
  By night and day my thoughts engage.
A broken statue, mildewed bust,
  Or rusty shield delights mine eyes ;
And Latin volumes thick with dust,
  Are treasures that I dearly prize.

Refrain.

I often wish that I had been
    A noble Roman ;
Had figured in some famous scene,
    A noble Roman ;
My triumphs both with pen and sword,
A bright example would afford ;
The world would cry with one accord—
    " A noble Roman !"

II.

Altho' I'm cast in modern mould,
  My inmost spirit is antique ;

Befitting best a Roman bold,
Or else a high poetic Greek.
Could I have twanged old Homer's lyre,
Or played on Virgil's oaten reed,
Or thrilled with Pompey's martial fire,
Ye gods! I had been blest indeed.

REFRAIN.

Behold me in a toga drest,
A noble Roman ;
My helmet crowned with lofty crest.
A noble Roman ;
Like Cicero's, my language flows.
I've Cato's gaze of stern repose,
And Julius Cæsar's eagle nose,
A noble *Roman !*

III.

Yet had my destiny so willed,
Had I in Rome first drawn my breath,
I might have been in battle killed,
And I prefer a natural death.
We moderns may have much to learn,
From those who flourished long ago.
But we might teach them in return
A thousand things they didn't know.

REFRAIN.

They lived for victory and strife,
Those noble Romans!
They littled valued human life,
Those noble Romans ;
Of stronger nerve than you or I,
Their custom was, I know not why,
To fall upon their swords and die
Like noble Romans !

No. 4.—SOLO.

Laura.

I.

When he is near, the woods are bright and green,
 The birds sing gaily on the trysting-tree ;.
The wind is soft, the azure sky serene,
 And every sight and sound is joy to me..
 For nothing can appear
 Unlovely, dull, or drear,
But all the world is beautiful when he is near.

II.

When he is gone, the woods are dark and sad,
 The birds sing mournfully, in plaintive pain ;
The wind is chill, no sunshine makes me glad,
 But gloomy clouds descend in tearful rain.
 Yet cease, sad heart, to fear,
 He will again be here,
And all the world is beautiful when he is near..

———

No. 5.—DUET..

Richie and Dolly.

I.

Rich.　If you love me and I love you,
 I don't see why we need disguise it ;
True love's a gem of purest hue,
 And as a treasure we should prize it..
So wherefore this pretended coldness ?
Rebuking your adorer's boldness ?
 Manner pettish,
 Words coquettish,
 Cannot grieve me,
 Or deceive me.

'Tis plain you love me, why not show it ?
I know it, and you know I know it.
DOLLY. Too openly we need not show it,
We don't want all the world to know it !

II.

DOLLY. If you love me and I love you,
  You say so, and I don't deny it ;
  If love's a gem of purest hue,
  No lover should too cheaply buy it.
  The heart that proves most worthy winning;,
  Seems hard when courtship is beginning..
    So though I'm pettish,
    And coquettish,
    Feign to leave you,
    Seem to grieve you.
Both. 'Tis plain you love me, for you show it,.
  I know it, and you know I know it.

No. 6.—" THE RAVEN AND THE DOVE."

(A Legend of Penraven Castle.)

DOLLY.

I.

In Saxon days an old sea rover,
  Who many a dauntless deed could boast,,
Had built a castle frowning over
  The summit of yon rock-bound coast.
His favourite raven—all folks knew it,
  An evil spirit (so they said)—
Survived him—till his widow slew it,
  And kept a gentle dove instead.

REFRAIN.

Pretty dove; so sweet to hear it,
  Cooing softly to its mate ;
Dreadful raven, how we fear it !—
  Harbinger of Woe and Fate !

II.

But time and change the work undoing
  Of those who reared the castle walls,
Have turned the tower to a ruin,
  And placed a stranger in its halls.
Penraven's line of lords has vanished,
  The last has left this earthly scene,
And dove and raven both are banished
  Among things that once have been ;
But should the brighter hour
  Resume it's welcome sway,
The dove will haunt the tower.
  The raven keep away.

REFRAIN. ,

Pretty dove, so sweet to hear it.
  Cooing softly to its mate ;
. Dreadful raven, come not near it,
  Harbinger of Woe and Fate !

No. 7.—SOLO.

HAROLD.

I.

How sweet the old familiar songs,
  My childhood loved to hear !
To each some memory belongs,
  Of byegone days so dear.
When life was full of fresh delights,
  And wonders new and strange,
And loving friends, and scenes and sights
  I thought would never change.

REFRAIN.

  Oh, sing the lays
  Of early days,
When sunshine on me smiled,
  Oh, wake for me the melody,—
  The sweet but simple melody,
That charmed me when a child !

II.

Y hear a long forgotten strain,
  An echo from the past ;
And vanished joys return again,
  I would they could but last !
The lips are mute that used to sing,
  The hands are still that played ;
Yet to my soul their numbers bring
  A charm that cannot fade.

REFRAIN.

  Oh, sing the lays
  Of early days,
When sunshine on me smiled ;
  Oh, wake for me the melody,—
  The sweet but simple melody,
That charmed me when a child !

No. 8.—CONCERTED PIECE.

DR. Q. Of Plutarch's lives I've had enough,
No more at present—*quantum suff.*
So now a teacher let me try
The rustic mind to edify.
Come forth, each blooming village lass,
To join my useful knowledge class.

Girls. We come, we come.
DR. Q.   Then form in line,
You hear ?
Girls.   We do.
DR. Q.   Your ears incline.
Attend !
Girls.   We will.
DR. Q.   Don't talk !
Girls.   We won't.
DR. Q. You understand me ?
Girls.   No, we don't.

Dr. Q. Beware the cane, the birch, the strap,
And don't provoke me—*verbum sap*.
If you'll attend to what I say,
I'll pilot you thro' learning's way.
Until the greatest ignoramus
For erudition shall be famous.
Now let me hear you spell Philippic.

1st. *Scholar.* F—I—L—

Dr. Q. That's not correct.   Begin it with a *P*..
Next, little number two
I must request of you
To conjugate the useful verb *To be*.

2nd. *Scholar.* *I am*.

Dr. Q.   That's right.

2nd. *Scholar.*   *Thou ammest*.

Dr.   No! No!

2nd. *Scholar.* *We is, You art, They be*.

Dr. Q.   Not so!
Oh, 'tis a dreadful task I find,
To educate the rustic mind.
Now let us all enjoy the fruits of learning,
Come, let us keep the lamp of Wisdom burning,
Leave farms and dairies, our milking and our
    churning :
Form a rural Universitee.
If fifty dozen sticks
Were sold for three-and-six,
    And these were burnt as fuel by the buyers,
Who wanted to obtain
That quantity again ;
    What would those sticks be sold for ?

1st. *Scholar.*   Why, for fires !

Dr. Q. Five from fifteen and what remains ?
I see you're cudgelling your brains.

Scholars. One ! One ! One ! One !

Dr. Q.   That cannot be.

Scholars. Yes, teacher, here it is you see !

Dr. Q. A dreadful task to train the rustic mind.

No. 8a.—MUSICAL FINALE.

CHORUS OF VILLAGERS.

CHO.   Seize the stranger ! There he stands,
        Up to mischief, we are sure ;
    Secret foes from foreign lands,
        Such as he, we can't endure.
    Gabriel has the evil eye,
        He's a wizard, well we know ;
    Fit companion for a spy,
        Let them both to prison go.

RICH.   Neighbours, why do you molest them ?
    What's the reason you detest them ?

Police.   Please, divide there,
        Stand aside there,
    We've a warrant to arrest them.

CHO.   They've a warrant to arrest them !

Police.   In the name of the law you are charged on
        suspicion,
    With being a spy of the French ;
    And please to remember, whatever admission,
        You make, we'll report to the Bench.

HAR.   Firmly I deny the charge,
        Zeal has carried you too far ;
    Set me instantly at large !

Police.   First inform us who you are.

HAR.   Your authority disputing,
    I refuse to give my name.

Police.   Then, our duty executing,
        We arrest you all the same.
    Gypsy Gabriel, we must take you.

GAB.   I'll not go.

Police.   The law will make you.

HAR.}   I protest, I protest,
GAB.}   I'll resist this arrest.

CHO.   They protest, they protest,
    They'll resist this arrest.

RICH.   If you will, I'll take your part,
        Not a bit of harm you've done ;
        Constable, you'd better start,
        Or, by Jove I'll give you one.

CON.   What resist the law? Beware!

RICH.   Certainly, I mean to fight ;
        Now arrest them if you dare,
        Friends and neighbours, am I right ?

CHO.   (*taking opposite sides.*) You're right!—You're
        wrong!
        You're right!—You're wrong!
        We'll aid the weak, !—We'll help the strong !

GRIM.
POLICE. $\begin{Bmatrix} \text{I} \\ \text{We} \end{Bmatrix}$ charge you all, who stand around,

        To take the part of $\begin{Bmatrix} \text{these} \\ \text{us} \end{Bmatrix}$ police,

        For you by penalties are bound
        To aid the the law and keep the peace.

COL.   What does this disturbance mean ?
LAURA.   In the purlieus of our dwelling ?
DOLLY.   'Tis a most disgraceful scene.
DR. Q.   Struggling, fighting, shouting, yelling.
        Who began it ? How or why
        It was started, there's no telling.

GRIM.   Capture Gabriel and the spy.

RICH.   You'll repent it if you try !

DOLLY.   Oh, my Richie, you are hurt !

RICH.   Not a bit, upon my word !

GRIM.   Give the rascals their desert.

COL.
DR. Q.   Could I make my questions heard,
        I might learn how this occurred.

GAB.   (*to* COL.) Your anger from this youth avert,
        'Tis Grimstone is your secret foeman ;

COL.   Give proofs of what you now assert ?

DR. Q.   I'll prove myself a noble Roman.

GRIM.
and
party.

Quick, secure them, every man ;
   Since persuasion won't avail,
We must try a bolder plan ;
   Take the culprits off to jail.

HAR.
RICH.
and
party.

You may catch us if you can,
   Your pursuit's of no avail ;
We have spoilt your little plan,
   Go and lock yourselves in jail.

TUTTI.

Now the warrant is destroyed,
   For another $\begin{Bmatrix} \text{we} \\ \text{you} \end{Bmatrix}$ must go ;
$\begin{Bmatrix} \text{Their} \\ \text{Our} \end{Bmatrix}$ arrest is null and void,
   Till authority $\begin{Bmatrix} \text{we} \\ \text{you} \end{Bmatrix}$ show.

END OF ACT 1.

ACT II.

No. 9.—CHORUS OF VILLAGERS.

The night is near, the sun has set,
But in the west there linger yet
  Some gleams of golden red ;
The bat begins his wayward flight,
The cloudy curtains of the night
  Are closing overhead.

Far down the road, so still and dark,
Each cottage shows a tiny spark,
  The lamp or firelight's glow ;
Such beacons guide our welcome way,
We've done to-day with work and play,
  So, neighbours, home we go.

No. 10.—DUET.

RICHIE and HAROLD.

RICH.   When lovers are not rivals too,
      Let each to each be friend and brother ;
    Content their chosen ones to woo,
      In sympathy with one another.
HAR.   For love is much the same to all,
      Whatever be their rank and station ;
    On willing ears its accents fall,
      In language needing no translation.

Both. You love, and so do I.
Our fortunes we will try,
In spite of angry guardians' frown and threat,
Perchance the serenade
I sing to my sweet maid
May blend with yours and form a fond duet.

No. 11 (*a*)—CHORUS OF SERVANTS.

Cho. Bolt the windows firm and tightly,
Draw the curtains close around,
Mind the keys are fitted rightly,
See the locks are safe and sound ;
Search the rooms till we are sure
Every place is quite secure ;
Master says it must be done,
He is such a cautious one.
He's afraid some prowling scamp,
Gypsy, poacher, thief, or tramp,
Never working, labour shirking,
In some corner may be lurking ;
Waiting till the house is still,
To perform some deed of ill.
Hark ! I thought I heard a noise !
There are robbers in the house ;

Men. We're prepared to fight 'em, boys.

Women. I'm as timid as a mouse.
Lord preserve us !—I shall cry !
I'm so nervous !—so am I.
I am fainting !—I shall scream !
I am dazed as in a dream !

Men. If you're frightened, take my arm,
You are trembling, I declare ;
What's the cause of this alarm ?
Lean upon my shoulder—there.

Women.	Thank you, I am better now,
	But I really can't allow
	Kisses pressed upon my brow,
	And your arms around me thus :
Men.	Well, I thought it not amiss,
	'Twas a very little kiss,
	No occasion for a fuss,
Dolly.	Goodness gracious ! what is this ?
Women.	They are taking care of *us.*
Dolly.	Here's the very deuce to pay !
	What on earth will master say ?
Cho.	We, in locking up the place,
	Heard some noises that alarmed us ;
Dolly.	Yes, but why in such a case
	Is it needful to embrace ?
Women.	Never mind, for no one harmed us.
Men.	'Twas their innocence that charmed us.
Dolly.	I am shocked beyond expression,
	You should act with more discretion.

(*b*)—SOLO.

Dolly.

I.

The men should be kept at a distance,
  Or else they are sure to grow bold ;
Meet every advance with resistance,
  Pretend to be scornful and cold.
Use kisses and smiles very sparely,
  Like gems from a limited store ;
For if you are gracious but rarely,
  They'll value your smiles all the more.

REFRAIN.

For love has no need to be always the same,
  A little cold water—a little cold water,
  A little cold water is good for the flame.

II.

To men the same rule I'm applying,
  Too fervent they should not appear ;
Not always be smiling or sighing,
  But sometimes look stern and severe,
'Tis foolish to show it too plainly,
  However you dote and adore ;
At times let her think she loves vainly,
  She'll value your smiles all the more.
                        [*Refrain as before.*

No. 12.—PATTER SONG.

DR. QUONDAM.

I.

A prodigy of learning, I am versed in every *ology*
  And deep in all the classics, whether Hebrew,
      Latin, Greek ;
At five years old I started on Comparative Philology,
  And read Egyptian obelisks as soon as I could speak,
At ten years old I'd mastered every system öf
      Astronomy,
  And knew the names and qualities of twenty
      million stars ;
I wrote a dissertation on the Book of Deuteronomy,
  And learnt a Hindoo treatise upon Jupiter and Mars.

REFRAIN.

Learning is a golden fount,
  Every one may drink of it ;
I must know a vast amount
  Now I come to think of it.

II.

I've studied hydrostatics, geognostics, and geology,
  I've solved in mathematics any problem that you
    please ;
Perused a Persian version of the Ninevite cosmogony,
  And paraphrased Confucius in pre-Adamite
    Chinese.
I'm quoted as an oracle on matters architectural,
  A critic on the Fine Arts who's invariably right ;
I'm most profound in logic and the sciences con-
    jectural,
  In metaphysic subtleties I take a deep delight.

[*Refrain.*

III.

I'm skilled alike in theories and practical appliances,
  No language comes amiss to me, no subject will I
    shirk ;
In point of fact I've travelled through the circle of the
    sciences,
  And I could *square the circle* if I chose to set to work.
I've learnt a hundred other things, with which I
    needn't trouble you,
  A perfect public library's established in my head ;
I know my cyclopædia from *A* right down to *W*,
  And must exhaust all learning by the time I get
    to *Z.*

[*Refrain.*

No. 13.—SOLO.

LAURA.

When thro' the heart the magic th,
  Of love has sealed our fate,
No stern decree, no tyrant's will,
  Can turn that love to hate ;
Its spell has power all else beyond,
  And cannot be undone,
The world can never break the bond
  That binds two hearts in one.

REFRAIN.

Love lives in joy, and dies in pain,
But while he lives, as king must reign.

II.

If time destroy the golden links
  That two fond hearts unite,
If love's fair star for ever sinks,
  And fades in endless night,—
Not all the might that monarchs own,
  Can mend that broken chain ;
No wizard, leagued with powers unknown,
  Can light that star again.

[*Refrain as*]

No. 14.—RECITATIVE.

HAROLD.

Ah, love, if I had wings,
  I'd spread them in delight ;
And leave all living things
  Behind me in my fli :

Har. ⎫	So swift o'er land and sea.
Rich. ⎭	I'd hasten unto thee.
Har.	My bark, on wings of white
	Hath borne me to this shore ;
	And stopped not day nor night.
	(My heart had flown before).
Har. ⎫	As messenger from me.
Rich. ⎭	And now I wait for thee.

BARCAROLLE.

I.

Har.   Come where the sunbeams are joyfully
glancing
  O'er the calm waters as blue as the sky ;
Home of bright sea-birds,—a picture entranc-
ing,
  Gaily my spirit within me is dancing,
    Hope fondly whispers " thy loved one is
nigh."

REFRAIN.

Har. ⎫	Ah come, ah come, I am waiting for thee !
Rich. ⎭	
Laura. ⎫	I come, I come, I have waited for thee !
Dolly. ⎭	Roam where thou wilt, it is heaven to me.

II.

Rich.   Come to yon island, all sunshine and flowers,
  A paradise set like a gem in the sea,
Where lovers may dwell in its fairy-like
bowers,
Forgetting the cares of this cold world of ours,
  Come, my adored one, I'm waiting for thee.

[*Refrain as before.*

No. 15.—CONCERTED PIECE.

LAURA. DOLLY.	'Tis you!
RICH. HAR.	'Tis I!
LAURA. DOLLY.	You've come at last,

When hope of seeing you had passed.
The time has moved with slow and weary wings,.
But oh! the boundless joy this moment brings.

LAURA.	But why so long away? A twelvemonth and a day, Leaving my heart to break!
RICH. DOLLY.	You make a great mistake; I saw you but two hours ago.
LAURA. HAR.	Ah no! Ah no!
DOLLY.	You've come again to plague my life,. And ask me if I'll be your wife..
HAR. RICH.	Say, what answer shall I get?. Am I doomed to joy or sorrow?'
DOLLY.	I have not decided yet, You may call again to-morrow.
HAR.	I am startled with surprise, At the tone of your replies.
All.	Voice and manner both are strange,. Strangers we have been too long ;. Have you undergone a change? Surely there is something wrong.. Have the goodness to explain ; We are in the light again.
LAURA. DOLLY.	What? 'tis you to me appealing!
HAR. RICH.	'Tis a blunder we discover, Both in wrong direction kneeling.
DOLLY.	Each has got the other's lover.
RICH.	Miss Tremaine, I ask your pardon, Most impertinent I seem ;

But I hope you'll not be hard on
  One who holds you in esteem.

LAURA. Least that's said, the soonest mended,
  You're forgiven.

RICH.   Lady, thanks!

DOLLY. Yes, but what if I'm offended?
  Recollect you're my intended,
    I am jealous at your pranks.

RICH. But the silly blunder's ended.

LAURA. I am longing to be told
  Where you've been and what you've done

HAR. Long the story to unfold,
  It would take till rise of sun;
  I have been an injured man,
    With my fortune 'neath a cloud:

DOLLY. Speak as softly as you can,
  Followers are not allowed.

ALL. Hark! good heavens! what was that?
  Footsteps coming to the door:
  Slippers going pit-a-pat,
    Like a cat along the floor,

Gracious $\begin{Bmatrix} \text{you} \\ \text{we} \end{Bmatrix}$ must not be seen,

Hide $\begin{Bmatrix} \text{them} \\ \text{us} \end{Bmatrix}$ quickly anywhere;

Hasten, get behind this screen,—
  Curtain—table—sofa—chair;
  Just in time, we've done it—there!

No. 16.—DUET.

HAROLD *and* LAURA.

I.

HAR. A chequered fate, dear love, is mine,
  A bird of passage have I been,
  O'er frigid zone and torrid line,
    To many a strange and distant scene.

A wanderer on the ocean waste,
　A pilgrim still I'm doomed to be ;
Ah ! would it were my lot to taste,
　The joys of home with love and thee !

Both.　But though a stern and cruel fate
　　May place us far as poles apart ;
'Our spirits cannot separate,
　For I am thine with all my heart.

II.

Laura.　A lonely life, dear love, I led
　The weary while thou wert away
I feared thee false, I deemed thee dead;
　And hope had fled for many a day.
The world could give me no delight,
　Nor pleasure soothe my secret pain ;
Now thou art here to bless my night,
　The sun begins to shine again.

Both.　But though a stern and cruel fate, &c.

No. 17.—FINALE TO ACT II.

Colonel *and* Chorus.

Cho.　Robbers here ! it's no delusion,
　. .　For we heard them very plain ;
Bringing uproar and confusion
　To the mansion of Tremaine.

Servants.　Gracious ! we're astounded, sir,
　.　Frightened and confounded, sir;
　　Strangers here, sir,
　　Very queer, sir,
　Mystery unbounded, sir.

Har.
Rich.　　If you look, you'll see that we
Laura.　Entered through the balcony.
Dolly.

Cho.	It was by the balcony.
Col.	Richie here, and Gabriel too ?
(*to* Har.)	Pray, sir, who the deuce are you ?'
Rich. } Har. }	We are honest people, Colonel.
Col.	·Very likely, on my word..
	Stealing here at hours nocturnal.
Cho.	Such impertinence infernal,
	Never have we seen or heard.
Har. } Rich. } Laura. } Dolly. }	Lovers true are one in heart,
	They are birds of kindred feather;
	And though strictly kept apart,
	Find a way to come together.
Col. (*angrily*)	Fiends and furies, fire and brimstone !
	Am I then deceived in Grimstone ?
Gab.	He's a villain and a traitor,
Laura.	He's a scheming calculator ;
Har.	He's a knave and parasite.
Rich.	He's a plotting Jacobite.
Cho.	He's a villain, &c.
Col.	You're in league with him, no doubt ;
	Servants, turn these strangers out.
Servants.	Out you go !
Rich., Har., *and* Gab.	This isn't right.
Servants.	Out you go !
Rich., Har., *and* Gab.	It's not polite.
Dr. Q.	Avaunt and quit us, Bedlamite,
Tutti.	Such unwarranted intrusion,
	Never shall occur again ;
	Causing uproar and confusion,
	In the mansion of Tremaine.

END OF ACT II.

ACT III.

No. 18.—CHORUS.

ENSEMBLE.

Midnight is the gypsy's noon,
  Though he loves the golden sun :;
Better still the silver moon,
  By her light his work is done.
Then it is that he arouses,
Lurks around the lone farm-houses ;
Then he takes the finest pickings
Of the roosting hens and chickens.
Ducks and geese and pigs purloining,
From the barns or yards adjoining,
In the game-preserves he rambles,
Shoots the rabbits at their gambols ;
Sets a snare for hare or pheasant,
Makes the traveller's route unpleasant,
Bursts upon him like a rocket,
Makes him empty every pocket !
    Ha ! ha ! ha !
When the smuggler creeps ashore,
  'Neath the dim and clouded moon ;
We are there to share his store,
  Midnight is the gypsy's noon.

No. 19.—SONG.

RICHIE.

I.

The smuggler is a bird of night,
  He wakes to life when daylight wanes,.
And lurks in clouded lunar light
  When stillness o'er the ocean reigns.
'Tis then the deeply-laden boat
  Is launched from out the anchor'd bark,.
To seek the rugged shore remote,
  Where lies the cavern deep and dark..

REFRAIN.

" A bold and reckless life is mine "—
  So runs the smuggler's toast ;
" Confusion on the Philistine,
  The guardian of the coast !"

II.

The smuggler, seen by common eyes,.
  No daring rover seems to be ;
To judge him by his outward guise,.
  A peaceful mariner is he.
But he has friends as well as foes,
  'Mid honest folks on sea and land ;
And many a cask of liquor goes
  Where no one knows 'tis contraband.

REFRAIN.

" A bold and reckless life is mine "
  Is still the smuggler's boast ;
" Confusion to the Philistine,
  The guardian of the coast ! "

No. 20.—COMIC TRIO.

DR. QUONDAM, LAURA, *and* DOLLY.

DR. Q.   Ladies, I'm your staunch protector,
         Strong as Samson, bold as Hector ;
         Thief or gypsy, ghost or spectre,
         I will fight if they appear.

LAURA. } While so gravely we're escorted,
DOLLY. } By your mighty arm supported,
         Every danger will be thwarted,
         We are safe while you are near.

Ensemble. { You } are safe while { I am } near.
            { We }   { you are }

DR. Q.   Oh dear, oh dear, they musn't hear !
         I quake with fear—I quake with fear,
         I'm not so bold as I appear.

LAURA.   I see 'twas a mad-headed whim
            To seek an adventure like this ;

DOLLY.   The Colonel—we're anxious for *him*,
            And that was the cause of it, miss.

DR. Q.   Fear not, fear not, you did quite rightly,
         This knight to-night will fight right knightly.
         My sabre may stick to its sheath,
            My musket may flash in the pan ;
         But still I am armed to the teeth
            And look like a dangerous man.

LAURA. } His sabre, &c.
DOLLY. }

         Doctor, though we're very frightened,
            In this dark and gloomy cave ;
         Still we feel our hearts are lightened,
            Led by one so true and brave,

DR. Q.   Valour is by peril heightened,
            I will both defend and save ;
         No occasion to be frightened,
            Led by one so true and brave.

(aside) If they notice how I'm trembling,
  They'll discover I'm dissembling.
(aloud) Hark, a footstep ! Shoulder arms !
  Ladies, get behind me there ;
  Nerve yourselves against alarms,
   None shall hurt you, I declare.
  Come forth, ye foes, that I may kill and slay !
(aside) I wish to goodness I could run away !

ENSEMBLE.

  Thus to face we know not what,
   Is a foolish error ;
  Yet we're rooted to the spot,
   In a mortal terror.

No. 21.—FINALE TO ACT III.

TUTTI.

Here's the end of doubt and danger,
  Pain and strife and absence long,
Welcome friend !—tho' once a stranger,
  Right has triumph'd over wrong !

Love has found a peaceful haven,
  On a bright and smiling shore,
And the Castle of Penraven
  Owns its rightful lord once more !

END OF OPERA.

BOOKS BY WALTER PARKE.

SONGS OF SINGULARITY.

Humorous Poems. Fifty Illustrations.

"Strikingly amusing."—*Standard.* "A fund of drollery and amusement."—*Morning Post.* "Exceedingly clever and entertaining."—*Literary World.* "Shows great versatility, and an unusually quaint and grotesque imagination."—*City Press.* "Whether grave or gay, it is always amusing."—*Bookseller.* "Irresistibly comic."—*Lloyd's.* "Displays remarkable ingenuity in the art of rhyming."—*Wigan Examiner.* "Bears the evidence of genuine humour and originality."—*Weekly Dispatch.* "Some of the illustrations possess considerable humour."—*Judy.* "Merrier conceits more neatly turned out we have not seen for a long time."—*South London Press.* "A humorist of singular talent and ingenuity."—*Dublin University Magazine.* "The book is deliciously comic, with touches of pathos in the graver portions, which remind us of Hood."—*Graphic.*

PEEPS AT LIFE.

Essays, Serious and Humorous.

Illustrated by GEORGE CRUIKSHANK.

"Shows much originality."—*Morning Post.* "Cleverly written, and pleasant reading."—*Standard.* "Will be appreciated for its bright and lively pages."—*Glasgow News.* "The essays are hit off in a happy vein."—*Bath and Cheltenham Gazette.* "This book contains the latest examples of Cruikshank's genius. . . . Pleasantly, wittily, and airily penned."—*Bookseller.* "Remarkable for correct thoughts, a fair style, and a certain subdued humour."—*Morning Advertiser.* "Most of the papers are very amusing."—*Saturday Review.* "Humorous, but not frivolous ; the 'London Hermit' is a close observer and a shrewd thinker."—*Figaro.* "I congratulate the author upon having secured the services of the Patriarch of the pencil to illustrate his amusing essays."—*Geo. Aug. Sala*, in the *Illustrated London News.*

LONDON : VIZETELLY & Co., 42, CATHERINE STREET, STRAND, W.C.

Price in cloth, gilt, 2s. 6d. each; in boards, 1s. each.

LAYS OF THE SAINTLY.

Burlesque Poems and Parodies.

Illustrated by JOHN LEITCH.

"Some of the poems are admirably adapted for public recitation."—*West Middlesex Observer*. "The stories are told in bright and luminous verses, into which are dexterously wrought parodies of past and present poets."—*Scotsman*. "Shows much facility in turning a verse."—*Graphic*. "Lovers of laughter, raillery, and things ludicrous, would do well to become possessed of this volume of humorous poems."—*Newcastle Chronicle*. "Mr. Walter Parke's versatility is marvellous. Tennyson, Poe, Whitman, Longfellow, Byron, Moore, he imitates with the utmost facility. His verses run easily. One may speak them trippingly from the tongue. Mr. John Leitch has furnished some humorous illustrations."—*Life*. "The verse is exceedingly clever, overflows with humour, and abounds with surprising turns of thought."—*Standard*. "We have had no such imitations of the idiosyncrasies of modern poets since the days of the gifted brothers, James and Horace Smith."—*Lady's Pictorial*.

PATTER POEMS.

Comic and Serious Verse, for Recitation.

Illustrated by JOHN LEITCH.

"We offer a cordial welcome to another delightful volume of verses by Mr. Parke. Whether humorous or serious, he is never dull. Many of the poems are well adapted for public reading or recitation."—*Literary World*. "A cleverly-written book of poems, both serious and humorous. They are decidedly above the average."—*Bath and Cheltenham Gazette*. "Of ' verbal volubility ' there are some amazing examples. Such poems as ' Arithmetical Posers ' will supply an endless fund of amusement to young people."—*Scotsman*. "Mr. Walter Parke, who has already achieved reputation from his comic opera of ' Estrella ' and from ' Les Manteaux Noirs,' has published an amusing collection of ' Patter Poems.'"—*Weekly Times*. "Both the comic and serious portions reflect the highest credit on the author. Bright fancy pervades the whole. In many cases it seems as if the mantle of poor H. S. Leigh had fallen upon Walter Parke."—*Lady's Pictorial*. "' Patter Poems ' include many sparkling and merry lays, well adapted for recitation, and sure of the approval of the audience."—*Saturday Review*.

LONDON: VIZETELLY & Co., 42, CATHERINE STREET, STRAND, W.C.

ERMINIE.

Comic Opera in Two Acts.

BY

PAULTON & JAKOBOWSKI.

LIST OF MUSIC.

		s.	d.
VOCAL SCORE - - - - - - -	nett	5	0
PIANO SCORE - - - - - - -	nett	2	6

VIOLIN AND PIANO.

			s.	d.
SELECTION - - Arranged by HENRY FARMER	nett	2	0

PIANO ARRANGEMENTS.

			s.	d.
MARCH - - - - - - - -	JAKOBOWSKI	nett	2	0
QUADRILLES - - - - - -	CHARLES COOTE	nett	2	0
WALTZES - - - - - - -	JAKOBOWSKI	nett	2	0
LANCERS - - - - - - -	Do.	nett	2	0
POLKA - - - - - - - -	Do.	nett	2	0
ENTR'ACTE GAVOTTE - - -	Do.	nett	1	6

VOCAL ARRANGEMENTS.

		s.	d.
"WHEN LOVE IS YOUNG." Song (Sop.) -	nett	2	0
"SIGHING SWAIN." Song (Sop.) - - - -	nett	2	0
DREAM SONG ("AT MIDNIGHT," &c.) Song (Sop.)	nett	2	0
"DARKEST THE HOUR." Song (Tenor) - -	nett	2	0
"LULLABY." Song (Sop.) - - - - - -	nett	2	0
"WHAT THE DICKY-BIRDS SAY" - - -	nett	2	0
"DOWNY JAILBIRDS OF A FEATHER" -	nett	2	0

LONDON: JOSEPH WILLIAMS.

PIANO COMPOSITIONS

BY

BRINLEY RICHARDS.

LONDON · JOSEPH WILLIAMS.

SONGS

COMPOSED BY

FLORIAN PASCAL.

<table>
<tr><td></td><td></td><td>s.</td><td>d.</td></tr>
<tr><td>1.</td><td>Dawn Song. Words by Reginald Barnett. Op. 17. No. 1. (Mezzo-Sop. or Bar.) ... ...</td><td>4</td><td>0</td></tr>
<tr><td>2.</td><td>Lady of the Day. Op. 17. No. 2. (Soprano)...</td><td>4</td><td>0</td></tr>
<tr><td>3.</td><td>Dreaming. Op. 17. No. 3. (Soprano) ... ...</td><td>4</td><td>0</td></tr>
<tr><td>4.</td><td>Bird of Day. Words by Fred. Enoch. Op. 18. No. 1. (Sop. or Mezzo-Sop.) ... ...</td><td>4</td><td>0</td></tr>
<tr><td>5.</td><td>Oh! by Rivers. Op. 18. No. 2. (Tenor) ...</td><td>4</td><td>0</td></tr>
<tr><td>6.</td><td>For you. Op. 18. No. 3. (Soprano) ... ...</td><td>4</td><td>0</td></tr>
<tr><td>7.</td><td>Love, I knew thee. Words by D. Christie Murray. Op. 19. No. 1. (Bar. or Mezzo-Sop.) ... ...</td><td>4</td><td>0</td></tr>
<tr><td>8.</td><td>A very old story. Words by D. Christie Murray. Op. 19. No. 2. (Sop. or Mezzo-Sop.) ... ...</td><td>4</td><td>0</td></tr>
<tr><td>9.</td><td>Glad my heart. Words by D. Christie Murray. Op. 19. No. 3. (Baritone) ... ...</td><td>4</td><td>0</td></tr>
<tr><td>10.</td><td>Dreaming in the Twilight. Words by Henry S. Leigh. Op. 20. No. 1. (Soprano) ... ...</td><td>4</td><td>0</td></tr>
<tr><td>11.</td><td>Divided. Words by Henry S. Leigh. Op. 20. No. 2. (Soprano) ... ...</td><td>4</td><td>0</td></tr>
<tr><td>12.</td><td>A Song to Portia. Words by D. Christie Murray. Op. 20. No. 3. (Mezzo-Sop.) ... ...</td><td>4</td><td>0</td></tr>
<tr><td>13.</td><td>On the sea shore. Words by Henry S. Leigh. Op. 21. No. 1. (Bar. or Contralto) ... ...</td><td>4</td><td>0</td></tr>
<tr><td>14.</td><td>O'er yon hill-tops. Words by Henry S. Leigh. Op. 21. No. 2. (Mezzo-Sop.) ... ...</td><td>4</td><td>0</td></tr>
<tr><td>15.</td><td>My bud in Heaven. Op. 21. No. 3. (Contralto) (With Violoncello Accompaniment.)</td><td>4</td><td>0</td></tr>
<tr><td>16.</td><td>The Jester's folly. Words by Mary Mark Lemon. Op. 30. No. 1. (Mezzo-Sop.) ... ...</td><td>4</td><td>0</td></tr>
<tr><td>17.</td><td>The Poet's theme. Words by Mary Mark Lemon. Op. 30. No. 2. (Mezzo-Sop.) ... ...</td><td>4</td><td>0</td></tr>
</table>

LONDON : JOSEPH WILLIAMS.

PIANOFORTE COMPOSITIONS

BY

W. KUHE.

No.		s.	d.
1.	Les Cloches de Corneville, 1st Fantasia	4	0
2.	Do. do. do. 2nd Fantasia	4	0
3.	Do. do. do. 3rd Fantasia	4	0
4.	The Ash grove (Welsh Melody)	3	0
5.	Singing thro' the rain (H. Smart)	3	0
6.	Souvenir de Prague	4	0
7.	Shells of Ocean (Transcription)	4	0
8.	O weel may the keel row	3	0
9.	La Gondola (Etude)	3	0
10.	Lass o'Gowrie (Scotch Song)	3	0
11.	Rosée du soir	3	0
12.	Scotch Airs (Fantasia de Concert)	4	0
13.	Silver threads	3	0
14.	Home, sweet Home (Transcription)	4	0
15.	Magic of Music (W. C. Levey)	4	0
16.	My lodging is on the cold ground	4	0
17.	Oh! dear, what can the matter be?	3	0
18.	Sun of my soul (Keble's Hymn)	3	0
19.	Ye happy birds (Transcription)	3	0
20.	Hark! the Vesper Hymn	3	0
21.	Weber's Last Waltz (Varied)	4	0
22.	Ye banks and Braes	3	0
23.	Bells of Aberdovey (Welsh Air)	3	0
24.	Caprice Bohemienne	4	0
25.	Bataclan (Offenbach)	4	0
26.	Barcarolle (Boatman's Return)	4	0
27.	Elfin home	3	6
28.	For a few days (Tully)	4	0
29.	Harp that once (Irish Air)	3	0
30.	Bold Marco	3	0
31.	Choeur de Chasse	3	0
32.	British Grenadiers March	3	0
33.	Cease your funning	3	0
34.	Captive Greek Girl	4	0
35.	Draw the Sword for Scotland	3	6
36.	Dermot Astore	4	0
37.	Danube River (Aide)	4	0
38.	L'Etoile du Nord (Meyerbeer	4	0
39.	Good-bye at the door (Glover)	4	0
40.	Within a mile of Edinboro' (Scotch Air)	3	0
41.	Pensées Musicales, Complete	5	0
42.	Sweetheart mine	3	0
43	L'Esperance (Esquisse)	3	0
44	Twelve Drawing Room Studies	6	

PIANOFORTE COMPOSITIONS,

BY

S. THALBERG.

No.		s.	d.
1.	HOME, SWEET HOME. Op. 72	3	0
2.	LAST ROSE OF SUMMER. Op. 73	4	0
8.	LUCREZIA BORGIA	4	0
4.	ANNA BOLENA. Op. 57	5	0
5.	AUF FLÜGELN DES GESANGES	3	0
6.	DON JUAN (La ci darem). Op. 14	6	0
7.	MINUET AND SERENADE ("Don Juan"). Op. 42	6	0
8.	DON PASQUALE. Op. 67	6	0
9.	L' ELISIR D' AMORE. Op. 66	6	0
10.	NORMA. Op. 57	4	0
11.	FERDINAND CORTEZ	3	0
12.	MELANGE SUR "EURYANTHE"	3	0
13.	CHARLES VI. (Halévy). Op. 48	5	0
14.	TRAVIATA. Op. 78	6	0
15.	TROVATORE. Op. 77	6	0
16.	IRISH AIRS. Op. 57	5	0
17.	GOD SAVE THE QUEEN. Op. 27	6	0
18.	LILLIE DALE. Op. 74	4	0
19.	GOD SAVE THE QUEEN (Simplified Edition). Op. 27	3	0
20.	SCHERZO. Op. 31	5	0
21.	WE'RE A' NODDIN	3	0
22.	SCHUBERT'S THREE MELODIES (Complete)	4	0
23.	DIE TAÜSCHUNG (Schubert)	1	6
24.	DIE NEUGIERIGE (Do.)	2	0
25.	DIE POST (Do.)	3	0
26.	FANTASIE. Op. 57	4	0
27.	COM' E GENTIL (Serenade). Op. 67	3	6
28.	SEMIRAMIDE. Op. 51	6	0

LONDON: JOSEPH WILLIAMS.

INSTRUMENTAL MUSIC.

COMPOSED BY SIR W. STERNDALE BENNETT.

JUST PUBLISHED.

SIR WILLIAM STERNDALE BENNETT'S Pianoforte Works,

in Two Volumes, 8vo. Edition, (paper covers) **6s.** net each.

(Handsomely bound in cloth) **8s.** net „

LONDON: JOSEPH WILLIAMS

LES CHARMES DE L'OPERA ITALIEN,

DUOS À QUATRE MAINS, POUR LE PIANO, PAR

J. RUMMEL.

PIANOFORTE DUETS.

LONDON: JOSEPH WILLIAMS.

POPULAR PIANO PIECES
By HAROLD THOMAS.

EXPLANATORY NOTE: A, very brilliant; B, brilliant, with moderate difficulty The leading fingering, and all necessary Directions for practice, marked throughout.

ORIGINAL PIECES, TRANSCRIPTIONS, ETC.

	s.	d.
Les Cuirassiers. Cavalcade Militaire ....A	4	0
The Sleigh-drive. Characteristic Piece ....A	4	0
Across Country-Chasse........A	4	0
Chant Bohemien...............A	4	0
Chant Rouman ....B	4	0
The Singing Fountain. Phantasy ....B	3	0
Birdie and Brooklet. Pastoral Idyll ....B	3	0
Air Styrien ....B	3	0
Transcriptions Brillantes. (D'apres Gounod):		
1. Chant de l'Ermite ....B	3	0
2. Valse Elegante............ B	3	0
3. Marche Nuptiale ....B	4	0
4. Grande Scene de Ballet B	4	0
Rhine Bells ....B	3	0
"Tho' short, decidedly sweet."—The Queen.		
Salzburg Chimes...............B	3	0
Au Tournoi. Marche Chevalresque ....B	3	0
The Musical Clock. Bagatelle. (Introducing Air of Louis XIII.) ....B	3	0

NATIONAL AIRS, ETC.

Albion. Introducing— Hearts of Oak, Home, sweet Home, The British Grenadiers	B	4	0
Erin. Introducing— The Minstrel Boy, Last Rose of Summer, St. Patrick's day	B	4	0
Scotia. Introducing— Auld lang syne, Blue Bells of Scotland, Campbells are comin'	B	4	0
Cambria. Introducing— Bells of Aberdovey, Poor Mary Ann, March, Men of Harlech	B	4	0

NATIONAL AIRS, ETC.—Cont.

	s.	d.
March of the Men of Harlech. (Easy Arrangement). Effect of Music in the distance ...	3	0
March of the Morgan Men. (Easy Arrangement).........	3	0

OPERATIC FANTASIAS, ETC.

Les Huguenots ....A	4	0
Faust. (Gounod) ....A	4	0
Lucia ....A	4	0
Mosè in Egitto. (The Prayer) A	4	0
Don Giovanni ....B	4	0
Der Freischutz ....B	4	0
Il Trovatore..................B	4	0
La Traviata ....B	4	0
Masaniello ....B	4	0
Stradella ....B	4	0
Marta.........................B	4	0
Lohengrin. (The Wedding Music) ....B	4	0
Tannhauser ....B	4	0
Le Prophete...................B	4	0
Les Cloches de Corneville ...B	4	0
Si j'etais Roi.................B	4	0

SACRED SUBJECTS.

St. Paul. (Mendelssohn) ......B	4	0
Hymn of Praise. (Mendelssohn) ....B	4	0
Cujus Animam. (Rossini's "Stabat Mater" ....B	4	0

DUETS.

Faust. (Gounod) ....B	5	0
Les Huguenots ....B	5	0
Chant Bohemien. (Easy bass, brilliant treble)	5	0
Au Tournoi. Marche Chevalresque ....B	4	0
The Sleigh-drive. Characteristic Piece ....B	4	0

"Among our English Pianists and Composers Mr. HAROLD THOMAS is taking a more and more prominent position—consequent on a more and more ample recognition of his rare qualities as an artist, the freshness, refinement, and elegance of his style. Mr. HAROLD THOMAS had recently the honour of being invited to perform before the Queen and Court at Windsor Castle, he played several compositions of his own, and was personally complimented in high terms."—Illustrated London News.

LONDON : JOSEPH WILLIAMS

NEW DRAWING-ROOM PIECES
BY
CH. NEUSTEDT.

N.B. — M., Moderate; M.D., Moderately Difficult.

TRANSCRIPTIONS CLASSIQUES.
(MORCEAUX DE CONCOURS.)
1re SERIE.

			s.	*d.*
1.	Romance de Weber	M.	2	0
2.	Sonatine de Beethoven	M.	2	6
3.	Les Saisons. Oratorio d'Haydn	M.	2	6
4.	La Romanesca. Air de danse XVI. Siècle ..	M.	2	6
5.	Andante de Mozart	M.	2	6
6.	Allegretto Agitato de la 2me. Symphonie de Mendelssohn	M.	2	6

(To be continued.)

CHEFS-D'ŒUVRE DRAMATIQUES ET LYRIQUES.
(DES GRANDS MAÎTRES.)

1.	Fantaisie Brillante, Oberon de Weber	M.D.	4	0
2.	,, ,, Egmont de Beethoven ..	M.D.	4	0
3.	,, ,, Sylvana de Weber	M.D.	4	0

TRANSCRIPTIONS VARIÉES, &c.

Fête Romaine. *Paladilhe*	M.D.	3	0
Chanson Napolitaine. Giulia Gentil	M.D.	3	0
Prière du soir. Meditation	M.D.	3	0
Sérénade de Zanetto. *Massenet*	M.D.	3	0
Chant d'Automne	M.D.	3	0
Havanaise. *Paladilhe*	M.D.	3	0
Célèbre Gavotte. *Gluck*	M.	3	0
Legende. Morceau Caracteristique	M.D.	3	0
Carnival Hongrois. Caprice Originale	M.D.	3	0
Première Tyrolienne Originale	M.D.	3	0
Plainte Moresque. *Bosch*	M.D.	3	0
Pasacalle. *Bosch*	M.D.	3	0
Retraite Espagnole. *Bosch*	M.D.	3	0
Air Anglais. Sweet Home. *Wrighton*	M.	3	0
Air Ecossais. Robin Adair	M.	3	0
Flower Song. Maiden's Flower Song. *Pinsuti* ..	M.	3	0
Carillon de Louis XIV.	M.	3	0
Don César de Bazan. *Massenet*	M.D.	3	0
Romance D'Arlequin. *Massenet*	M.D.	3	0
Nuit D'Espagne. *Massenet*	M.D.	3	0
Fantasia brillante sur Gretna Green	M.D.	4	0
A Rustic Wedding. A Sketch	M.D.	3	0

LONDON · JOSEPH WILLIAMS.

PETITES
SOIRÉES MUSICALES,

SIX MORCEAUX MIGNONS, POUR PIANO ET VIOLON,

ARRANGÉS PAR MAURICE LEE.

PIANO ET VIOLON CONCERTANTS.

FAVOURITE DUETS,
FOR
VIOLIN AND PIANO.

N.B.—M. moderate; M.D. mod. diff.; D. difficult.

LONDON : JOSEPH WILLIAMS.

"ECHOES OF THE PAST."

THIRTY INSTRUCTIVE DUETS, FOR VIOLIN AND PIANO, ARRANGED BY

HUBERT RIES.

No.

Two Shillings and Sixpence each.

By HENRY FARMER.

LONDON: JOSEPH WILLIAMS.

POPULAR DANCE MUSIC.

BY

FAVOURITE COMPOSERS.

WALTZES.

		s. d.
Ada	Henry Farmer	4 0
Alarm	C. H. R. Marriott	4 0
Alma	H. Weist Hill	4 0
As You Like It	J. Püchter	4 0
Babiole	Arban	4 0
Billee Taylor	C. Godfrey	4 0
Cloches de Corneville	O. Metra	4 0
Cloches de Corneville	E. Deransart	4 0
Dawn of Day	Henry Farmer	4 0
Donna Juanita	E. Strauss	4 0
Duchess	Henry Farmer	4 0
First Love	Henry Farmer	4 0
Grand Casimir	O. Metra	4 0
Kathleen	C. H. R. Marriott	4 0
Lalla Rookh	Lambert	4 0
Laura	W. Hemin way	3 0
Laura	Henry Farmer	4 0
Love Bird	C. H. R. Marriott	4 0
Lily	Charles Coote, Jun.	4 0
Maids of Merry England	H. Farmer	4 0
Mama's Pet Waltz	Henry Farmer	4 0
Marion	Charles Coote, Jun.	4 0
Mina	Charles Coote, Jun.	4 0
Naval Cadet	Graziani	4 0
Passion Flower	Charles Coote, Jun.	4 0
Princess Beatrice	C. H. R. Marriott	4 0
La Petite Mademoiselle	A. Grenville	4 0
Bon Image	H. Weist Hill	4 0
Snowdrops	Charles Coote, Jun.	4 0
Susanne	A Grenville	4 0
True Love	H. Weist Hill	4 0
Wild Briar	Henry Farmer	4 0

POLKAS.

		s. d.
Abbotsford	J. G. Jones	3 0
Ariel	C. H. R. Marriott	3 0
Arm-in-Arm	Ph. Fahrbach	3 0
A Ton Bras	T. Rieffier	3 0
Babiole	O. Metra	3 0
Belle of the Promenade	Weist Hill	3 0
Belle Vue	W. Smallwood	3 0
Billee Taylor	A. Grenville	3 0
Bon Bon	C. E. Tinney	3 0
Captive	C. H. R. Marriott	3 0
Cloches de Corneville	Arban	4 0
Colombine	Ph. Fahrbach	3 0
Devonshire	Madame Oury	3 0
First Ball	Stagg	3 0
First Kiss	Henry Farmer	3 0
First Step	C. H. R. Marriott	3 0
Gertrude	H. Weist Hill	3 0
Hesperus	E. Strauss	3 0
Inverness	C. Morine	3 0
Joliette	Tom Brown	3 0
Merry Midnight	Henry Farmer	3 0
Minna	W. Hemingway	3 0
Picnic	J. Pridham	3 0
Naval Cadets	A. Grenville	3 0
Rose of the Valley	Henry Farmer	3 0
Salerno	W. Smallwood	3 0
Skating	W. V. Wallace	4 0
Ting-ting	J. Püchter	3 0
Tout a la Joie	Ph. Fahrbach	3 0

QUADRILLES.

		s. d.
Argyle	C. H. R. Marriott	4 0
Babiole	Arban	3 0
Billee Taylor	Charles Coote, Jun.	4 0
Christmas (Arranged for Small Hands)	Henry Farmer	2 0
Cloches de Corneville	C. Coote, Jun.	4 0
Cloches de Corneville	Arban	4 0
Cloches de Corneville	O. Metra	4 0
Donna Juanita	Chas. Coote, Jun.	4 0
Empress	Henry Farmer	4 0
Gorilla	C. H. R. Marriott	4 0
Grand Casimir	Arban	4 0
International	C. H. R. Marriott	4 0
Juno	Henry Farmer	4 0
Lady of Lorne	C. Godfrey	4 0
La Petite Mademoiselle	Marx	4 0
La Petite Mademoiselle	Arban	4 0
Little Fairies	Henry Farmer	3 0
Midsummer	Henry Farmer	3 0
Naval Cadets	E. Strauss	4 0
Orphée aux Enfers	E. Strauss	3 0
Parisienne	H. Hemy	3 0
Pet Doves	W. Smallwood	3 0
Salerno	C. H. R. Marriott	4 0
Scotland	J. T. Stone	3 0

LANCERS.

		s. d.
Babiole	A. Grenville	4 0
Billee Taylor	A. Grenville	4 0
Cloches de Corneville	A. Grenville	4 0
Duke of Edinburgh	H. Hemy	4 0
Grand Casimir	A Grenville	4 0
Naval Cadets	A. Grenville	4 0
Petite Mademoiselle	A. Grenville	4 0

GALOPS.

		s. d.
Babiole	A. Grenville	3 0
Bashi-Bazouk	H. Weist Hill	3 0
Belle Vue	W. Smallwood	3 0
Carillon	T. Riviere	3 0
Crazed	E. Solomon	3 0
Cloches de Corneville	A. Grenville	4 0
Flirtation	J. G. Jones	3 0
Flora	H. Farmer	3 0
Gorilla	C. H. R. Marriott	3 0
Jog Trot	Tom Brown	3 0
Lady of Lorne	C. Godfrey	4 0
Lillian	W. Hemingway	3 0
Moss Trooper	H. Hemy	4 0
No Thoroughfare	Chas. Coote, Jun.	3 0
Owl	C. H. R. Marriott	3 0
Prince Imperial (100th Thousand)	Chas. Coote, Jun.	4 0
Skedaddle	C. Money	3 0
Strasburg	A. Mullen	3 0
Tandem	Henry Farmer	4 0
Tantivy	J. P. Clarke	3 0
To Paris	H. Weist Hill	3 0
Tramp, Tramp	C. Money	3 0
Tramway	Charles Coote, Jun.	3 0

LONDON: JOSEPH WILLIAMS.

Violin, and Violin and Piano Music.

HENRY FARMER.

	s.	d.
CELEBRATED VIOLIN SOLOS, on Popular Airs, with Pianoforte Accompaniments............each	3	0

No. 1. Home, sweet Home.
2. Last Rose of Summer.
3. Blue Bells of Scotland.
4. Life let us cherish.
5. Hope told a Flattering Tale.
6. The Harp that once.
7. The Keel Row.
8. Swiss Air, and Gentle Zitella.
9. Sounds so Joyful, (from 'Sonnambula.')

FANTASIA on Airs from PLANQUETTE's Popular Opera, 'Les Cloches de Corneville'...................	4	0
SONATINA, in G. No. 1	5	0
SONATINA in C. No. 2	5	0
LARGO (Handel)	3	0
GAVOTTE (Rameau)	3	0

HENRY G. BLAGROVE.

SIX VIOLIN SOLOS, on Popular Airs, Composed and Arranged in a Progressive Style, with the Fingering marked, and an Accompaniment for the Pianoforte ....each	4	0

No. 1. Fantasia on 'Logie o' Buchan,' and 'My Boy Tammie.'
2. Variations on Air by Himmel.
3. Rondo on 'The Plough Boy,' and 'Rousseau's Dream.'
4. Rondo on 'The Jolly Young Waterman.'
5. Introduction, 'The Last Rose of Summer,' and Rondo on 'While the Lads of the Village.'
6. Fantasia on 'Don Giovanni,' introducing 'Vedral Ca ino,' and 'Fin ch' han da! Vino.'

The above are also published as Violin Duets.

SOUVENIRS.—Six Solos for Violin, with Pianoforte Accompaniment:—

No. 1. La Figlia	4	0
2. Welsh Airs	5	0
3. Scotch Airs	5	0
4. Il Flauto Magico..........	5	0
5. Irish Airs	5	0
6. La Donna del Lago........	6	0
CELEBRATED VIOLIN SCALES. In Three Books each	3	0
A GERMAN AIR. In D	3	0
A GERMAN AIR. In G...........	3	0
CLASS MUSIC, being a Series of Educational and Progressive Studies, arranged as Solos, Duets, Trios, Quartetts, and Quintetts, with Viola and Violoncello parts ....each	2	0

ADOLPHE HERMANN.

FANTASIA on Airs from 'Les Cloches de Corneville'....................	3	0
PAVANE—BRISSON	3	0

SIEGFRIED JACOBY.

	s.	d.
POPULAR AIRS for Violin and Piano. ....each	2	8

No. 1. Home, sweet Home.
2. Santa Lucia.
3. Serenade, Wekerlin.
4. Silver Threads among the Gold.
5. O Catarina Bella.
6. The Minstrel Boy.

LEOPOLD JANZA.

GEMS OF THE OPERA. A Selection of Melodies. With an Accompaniment for the Pianoforte .. each	3	0

No. 1. La Sonnambula (Bellini).
2. Il Pirata.
3. L'Elisire D'Amore (Donizetti).
4. Lucrezia Borgia.
5. Euryanthe (Weber).
6. Stradella (Flotow).
7. La Part du Diable (Auber).
8. Il Furioso (Donizetti).
9. Die Matrosen (Flotow).

FLORIAN PASCAL.

PENSEES CELTIQUES	5	0

E. NORMAN.

BALMORAL. Brilliant Fantasia on Scotch Airs.....................	6	0

E. PERIER.

LES BERGERS WATTEAU. Fantasia on L. Gregh's Popular Dause..		

CHARLES TOURVILLE.

FAVOURITE SUBJECTS ......each	3	0

No. 1. Phillis (a la Gavotte).
2. She wore a W eath of Roses.
3. Chant du Soir
4. Carnival de V nice.
5. I love my Love.
6. The Dream (Haydn).
7. Gavotte, Louis XIV.
8. Serenade du Passant (Massenet).
9. Robin Adair.
10. Mary of Argyle.
11. Rigaudon du Dardanus (Rameau).
12. Serenade (Marschan).

'LES CLOCHES DE CORNEVILLE.' The Complete Opera arranged for Violin Solo ....net	2	0
Ditto for Second Violin ... .net	2	0

N.B.—These Books are Arranged expressly for use with the Pianoforte Score.

VARIOUS (Violin only).

LEO.—The Celebrated CUCKOO SOLO	1	6
„ FARMYARD SOLO	1	6
POUSSE.—THE CAT'S MINUET	1	0

LONDON: JOSEPH WILLIAMS.

NEW SACRED CANTATA,

JACOB.

COMPOSED BY

HENRY SMART.

THE WORDS COMPILED FROM HOLY SCRIPTURE BY

J. C. C. McCAUL.

Vocal Score, complete, 8vo.	..	..	..	..	4s. nett.
Ditto,	ditto,	bound	..	..	..	6s. nett.

The Vocal and Orchestral Parts are published, and may be had. The most popular Numbers of the Cantata are published separately.

NEW SACRED CANTATA,

MARIE MAGDELEINE.

BY

JULES MASSENET.

Vocal Score	..	..	..	..	..	4s. nett.

ENGLISH VERSION BY

HENRY S. LEIGH.

London: JOSEPH WILLIAMS.

𝔑aaman, an 𝔒ratorio.

By SIR MICHAEL COSTA.

THE WORDS SELECTED AND WRITTEN BY

WILLIAM BARTHOLOMEW.

		s. d.
Vocal Score, complete, folio. Handsomely bound	.. .. ..	**15s.** rett
Ditto People's Edition, 8vo. Paper covers	.. .. ..	**4s.** „
Ditto Ditto Bound cloth	.. .. ..	**6s.** „
Orchestral Score	.. ..	**£8 8s.** „

Orchestral Parts to be had separate.

ARRANGEMENTS.

			s. d.
WILLIAM HUTCHINGS CALLCOTT. Selection of Airs. Books 1 & 2 .. each			5 0
W. J. WESTBROOK. Triumphal March. Organ			3 6
SIR MICHAEL COSTA. Ditto Piano Solo			3 0
Ditto Ditto Piano Duet			4 0

RIMBAULT, E. F. Arrangements for the Harmonium :—

London : JOSEPH WILLIAMS

Eli, an Oratorio.

By SIR MICHAEL COSTA.

THE WORDS SELECTED AND WRITTEN BY

WILLIAM BARTHOLOMEW.

Vocal Score, complete, folio. Handsomely bound	..	..	..	15s. net
Ditto People's Edition, 8vo. Paper covers	..	..	..	4s. "
Ditto Ditto Bound cloth	..	..	..	6s. "
Orchestral Score,	..	..	..	..	..	£3 3s. "

Orchestral Parts to be had separate.

PART I.

No.		s.	d.
1 Overture		8	0
2 Recit. Blow up the trumpet ..	}	4	0
3 Chorus. Let us go to pray			
4 Recit. Behold!	}	8	0
5 Air with Chorus. Let the people			
6 Chorus. Blessed be the Lord ..		8	0
7 Recit. Unto Thee, O Lord	}	8	0
8 Prayer. Turn Thee unto me ..			
9 Recit. Woman, how long	}	8	0
10 Chorus. The Lord is good ..			
11 Recit. Hannah, why weepest ..	}	8	0
12 Duetto. Wherefore is my soul ..			
13 Chorus. For every thing ..		6	0
14 Recit. My sons!	}	9	0
15 Air. If thou should'st mark ..			
16 Chorus O ye kindreds	}	8	0
17 Recit. I am come			
18 Solo and Chorus. Philistines, hark!	}	8	0
19 Air. Hear my prayer			
20 Recit. Eli, thus saith the Lord..	}	8	0
21 Duetto. Lord, cause Thy face ..			
22 Chorale. O make a joyful noise			
23 Solo. The Lord is in His holy temple	}	8	0
24 Recit. Open unto me ..	}	8	0
25 Air. I will extol Thee, O Lord ..			

PART I.—continued.

No.		s.	d.
26 Recit. Why camest thou			
27 Solo and Chorus. Blessed is he..	}	8	0
28 Chorus. Hosanna!			

PART II.

No.		s.	d.
29 The Morning Hymn. Lord, from my bed	}	8	0
30 Recit. My mother, bless me ..	}	8	0
31 Trio. Thou shalt love the Lord			
32 Solo. Go in peace	}	8	0
Quartett. We bless you			
33 March of Israelites		8	0
34 Recit. Hear, O Israel	}	4	0
35 Chorus. Hold not thy peace ..			
36 Recit. It is a good thing ..			
37 The Evening Prayer. This night I lift	}	8	0
38 Chorus of Angels. No evil shall		8	0
39 Recit. and Chorus. Woe unto us,	}	4	0
40 for we are spoiled ..			
41 Recit. When shall I arise	}	8	0
42 Chorus. Bless ye the Lord ..			
43 Recit. I wait for the Lord ..	}	8	0
44 Air. Although my house.. ..			
45 Chorus. Lament with a doleful..		8	0
46 Recit. What meaneth the noise			
47 Chorus. The glory is departed ..	}	8	8
48 Chorus. Blessed be the Lord ..			
49 Chorus. Hallelujah! Amen ..			

PIANO ARRANGEMENTS.

WILLIAM H. CALLCOTT. Selection of Airs. (Two books) ..	..	each	5	6
Ditto ditto ditto as Duets. (Two books)	"	6	0
Ditto The Morning Prayer		2	6
Ditto ditto Duet		8	0
Ditto The Evening Prayer	..	2	6
Ditto ditto Duet	..	8	0
CHARLES LUCAS. March of Israelites. Solo or Duet ..	..	each	8	0
THE MARCH. Arranged as a Pianoforte Trio			4	0

ORGAN ARRANGEMENTS.

By Dr. G. T. CHIPP.

	s.	d.			s.	d.
Overture	8	0	March (With pedal obligato) ..		8	0
Morning Prayer	2	0	Blessed be the Lord..		2	0
Evening Prayer	2	0	If thou should'st mark		2	0
Woe unto us. (Chorus)	2	0	Hallelujah. (Chorus)		2	0

Dr. E. F. RIMBAULT. Principal Airs for Harmonium, 8vo. Bound paper ..		4	0
THE MARCH. Arranged for the Harmonium		8	0
" " As Septett	nett	1	0
" " Full Orchestra	nett	2	0

"MARCH ONWARD." The celebrated March of the Israelites. Arranged as a Four-part Song. Price 6d. Separate Vocal Parts 3d.

London: JOSEPH WILLIAMS.

SUZANNE.

OPERA IN THREE ACTS.

COMPOSED BY

E. PALADILHE.

WORDS ADAPTED FROM THE FRENCH OF

MM. LOCKROY AND CORMON

BY

HENRY S. LEIGH.

LONDON: JOSEPH WILLIAMS.

OPERA BOOKS.

LES CLOCHES DE CORNEVILLE. Lyrics only. By R. REECE and H. B. FARNIE. Three Acts.

LA PETITE MADAMOISELLE. Complete Libretto. By H. S. LEIGH and R. REECE. Three Acts.

BABIOLE. Complete Libretto. By R. REECE. Three Acts.

THE GREAT CASIMIR. Complete Libretto. By H. S. LEIGH. Three Acts.

LA JOLIE PERSANE. Complete Libretto. H. S. LEIGH and R. REECE. Three Acts.

DON ANTONIO. Complete Libretto. By H. S. LEIGH and MACKENZIE. Three Acts.

SUZANNE. Complete Libretto. By H. S. LEIGH. Three Acts.

CUPS AND SAUCERS. Complete Libretto and Music. By GROSSMITH. One Act.

BLIND BEGGARS. Complete Libretto and Music. H. B. FARNIE. One Act.

BREAKING THE SPELL. Complete Libretto and Music. By H. B. FARNIE. One Act.

CLAUDE DUVAL. Lyrics only. By H. P. STEPHENS. Two Acts.

CYMBIA. Complete Libretto By HARRY PAULTON. Three Acts.

CYMBIA. Lyrics Only. By HARRY PAULTON. Three Acts.

BILLEE TAYLOR. Lyrics Only. By H. P. STEPHENS. Two Acts.

LORD BATEMAN. Lyrics only. By H. P. STEPHENS. Two Acts.

HIS ONLY COAT. Complete Libretto and Music. By J. DALLAS. One Act.

LADY LAURA'S LAND. Complete Libretto. By W. F. BROUGHTON. One Act.

CAPTAIN OF THE GUARD. Complete Libretto. By G. FOX. Two Acts.

LAURETTE. Lyrics only. By H. S. LEIGH.

VICAR OF BRAY. Complete Libretto. By SYDNEY GRUNDY.

LONDON: JOSEPH WILLIAMS.

www.ingramcontent.com/pod-product-compliance
Lightning Source LLC
Chambersburg PA
CBHW031801090426
42739CB00008B/1106